WORI

THE BANSTE

by

JOHN SWEETMAN

A PUBLICATION BY

THE BANSTEAD HISTORY RESEARCH GROUP

1995

ISBN 0 9512741 2 0

Typeset, printed and bound by
The Print Centre, Epsom, Surrey.

PREFACE

This is the story of a camp which existed at Park Farm in Holly Lane during and for some time after the Second World War.

The main facts emerged from enquiries made by the Group two or three years ago. This resulted in a flood of information from people living locally, including, most unexpectedly, a reply from someone well-known in the village for a number of years. He proved to have been a prisoner-of-war in the camp in 1946-7.

The Group's book, 'Banstead: a History', published in December 1993, contained a chapter about Banstead in the War years, with a brief reference made to the camp. Now it is possible to give a more detailed history of the camp.

The Group acknowledges with thanks the help given by all those who provided the information on which this story is based. A few of them, to whom particular thanks are due, are mentioned in the note of sources at the end of the text. If what is said here arouses in readers other memories about the camp or its occupants, we shall be glad to hear from them.

CONTENTS

ILLUSTRATIONS

1. BANSTEAD WOODS BEFORE THE WAR

When the Second World War broke out in 1939, most of the Banstead Woods was open to the public, having been acquired by the Surrey County Council under the Green Belt legislation which had come into force a few years earlier. The mansion in the heart of the woods, which had been the home of the wealthy Garton family from 1893 until the death of Mr. Garton senior in 1934, had, along with its immediate grounds, been excluded from the pruchase by the County Council. In 1937 it had been conveyed to trustees for a Children's Hospital which was to be set up there.

Included in the property acquired by the County Council was an old house near Holly Lane, on the northern side of the entrance road to what is now known as Park Farm, beyond the flint-walled barn which remains there today. Until the mansion in the woods was built in the 1880s for the Hon. Francis Baring, this house had been the main residence on the Banstead Wood estate. It had been variously known as 'Banstead Park', 'Park Wood House' or 'Banstead House'. Also included in the property acquired by the County Council were the Lodge at the entrance and the two cottages on the southern side of the Lodge. These are said to have been provided for the butler and the gardener at the mansion. The Long Barn and round flint-walled barns (one of which lay just beyond the Long Barn) were also acquired by the County Council at this time.

Park Farm and Banstead Wood House.

The Round Barn
near the Entrance Road.

2. THE WOODS IN WARTIME

From the beginning of the War and until two years after its end, most of the Banstead Wood estate was occupied under requisitioning powers by the War Department, and the public was excluded from the woods. By 1940 anti-invasion works were in place on the edges of Holly Lane. There were anti-tank ditches, short concrete pyramids known as 'dragon's teeth', and a strongpoint in the field above the Long Barn. Later the mansion in the woods was turned into a temporary military hospital.

3. THE CANADIAN CAMP

The area round the old house and the Long Barn was in 1940 converted into a camp for Canadian troops, who were arriving in the country in large numbers. Most of them were being stationed in the southern counties, many of them in Surrey. A number of huts were built in the area, for use as living quarters, storehouses and so on, and the existing buildings, such as the Lodge, were allocated for various purposes.

The camp stretched out into the woods themselves, which provided cover for vehicles, guns and ammunition, as well as for tents for the troops. The Sergeants' Mess and the Corporals' Mess were housed in the cottages adjoining the Lodge, which was used as the Guard House.

A young lady (now Mrs. Stella Hayward), who lived in Court Hill, Chipstead, helped to run a Y.M.C.A. canteen which was set up by volunteers in the old house at the camp.

She kept a diary in which she recorded memories of these times.   They are pleasant memories in spite of their background of air raids, wartime shortages, and the difficulties and dangers of commuting to London to work.

She found the Canadians "friendly, jokey and outgoing".   Some of them were camping out under canvas in the woods themselves, under quite primitive conditions, as the winter of 1940-41 came on.   Passers-by could see them shaving in the open air, with a mirror nailed to a tree.   Householders nearby formed a "rota" to provide them with an occasional hot bath.   The woods also "concealed row upon row of army vehicles and ammunition".

Discipline in the camp was more relaxed than in a British camp.   There was a large notice which read "No saluting in this camp".

Many other Canadians were accommodated in other places in and around Banstead - for example, in huts in Nork Park, and in houses in Chipstead.   They were lively and occasionally rumbustious.   They made many friends, and a few of them married local girls.   Those in the Banstead Wood Camp were mostly from the Royal Canadian Engineers, the Royal Canadian Regiment and the Royal Canadian Artillery.   They were "full of energy and joie de vivre, and uninhibited".   Female company was a delight, and they loved dancing, particularly 'barn dancing'.   This was carried on, appropriately enough, in the Long Barn.   The Canadians taught the local girls barn dancing, and literally swept them off their feet.   They held dances in other places, too.   On Canada Day there was a dance at the Netherne Hospital, after which they walked the helpers back to their homes in Chipstead and Coulsdon.

The canteen in the camp was "very cosy, chintz curtains, flowers etc., a nice fire, chairs and a settee". It occupied the ground floor and the first floor of the old house. There was a piano and room for dancing and for table tennis. Officially there was no alcohol on the premises. When Stella toured the tables after the soldiers had come into the canteen for tea and sandwiches, offering to 'top-up' their tea-cups, she soon realised that many of the cups had already been topped-up - with whisky! But there was no drunkenness in the canteen, and complete honesty. When there was a rush of customers, the men would take their own change from the till, and nothing was lost.

Over the next three years the Canadian troops came and went, and the girls in the canteen made good friends amongst them and shared with them the wartime hazards and discomforts, such as those from the frequent air-raids. Sometimes these made it difficult or dangerous to get to and from the canteen. A few entries from the diary in November and December 1940 illustrate the sort of situations which they encountered, and how they faced up to them:

20 November 1940   To canteen.   V. merry time with fellow playing concertina v. well & everyone singing. I was escorted home (Raid as usual) by Robert Taylor. (I had to see his card before I believed him!). Gunfire terrific & just after I donned the tin hat, a shellcap dropped on the road behind us. The flashes were blue like lightning.

5 December 1940	7.30. Heard a German plane v. low, so I ran out on to the lawn. Heard a H.E. drop (between Viaduct & Dene Farm) - our local guns opened up & I saw 2 Molotov breadbaskets drop 200 incendiaries in all from Old Oak on the railway line and up Hazelwood Lane, across Walpole Ave. to Chipstead Village. Whole countryside lit by green glare for abt. ½hr. - I cd. have read by it. After all that no house burnt or person hurt. We brought down both planes.
18 December 1940	Canteen - when we closed 10.00 a raid was on. So we were all ordered into truck that wd. deliver us back home. I sat beside the driver & he gave me a box of matches which he said I was to light when he said. So each time he changed gear I had to light a match. His driving was so erratic, we got to Coulsdon alright - but I being last, told him not to take me up Court Hill (I didn't think he'd make it!). Then he tells me he's a motorcyclist and never driven a car before, let alone a truck - those Canadians make you laugh!

A special occasion was the Canteen party at Christmas 1940. This was a dance and show put on by the Canadians. Half an hour was allowed for the show, with a variety of turns. Then at half-past-seven, the hall was cleared, and everybody - about 50 men and 8 girls - danced until after midnight. Every dance was an "Excuse-me" dance, and the girls never stopped dancing.

PARK FARM.

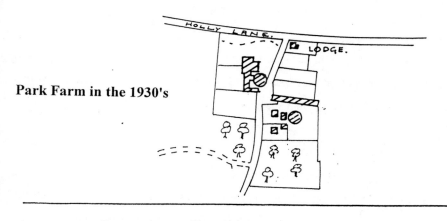

Park Farm in the 1930's

LODGE.

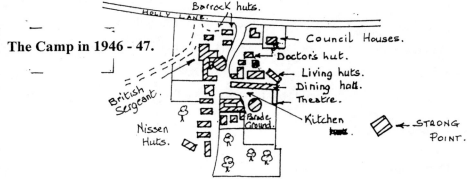

The Camp in 1946 - 47.

Barrack huts.
Council Houses.
Doctor's hut.
Living huts.
Dining hall.
Theatre.
Kitchen.
STRONG POINT.
British Sergeant.
Nissen Huts.
Parade Ground.

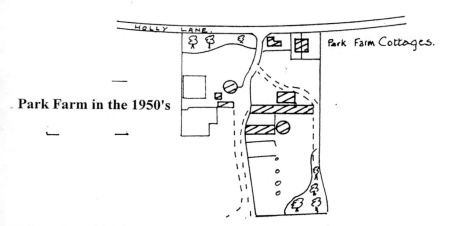

Park Farm in the 1950's

Park Farm Cottages.

11.

"The square dances were terrific, when they swung you round till your feet left the floor and you were circling round with your feet level with your head.".

The girls who worked in the canteen had their full share of the downside of wartime; but for them it was balanced by the great fun and comradeship which they enjoyed with the Canadian soldiers.

As the War turned in favour of the Allies, the air raids died down. Preparations were beginning for the invasion of Europe, in which the Canadians would play a prominent part. Then the "flying bombs" began to fall. An extract from the diary for 15th of June 1944 reads: "P.M. To the Canteen. I'm afraid my Canadians may go now - they are all ready. I just love them all - such friendly, humorous and loveable people. I can't imagine the Canteen without their bantering and whimsical humour ...... That night we had 112 buzzers (flying bombs) over our sector and the explosions shook the house. I gave up trying to sleep and read a book instead".

In fact, nearly all the Canadians left the Banstead Wood Camp on the 10th of July 1944, and the diary for Friday, the 14th July, sadly records: "To the Canteen. All my Canadians gone. They moved off at 4.00 a.m. on Monday - a convoy 2½ miles long. Banstead Woods must have hidden vast quantities of stores, ammunition, guns, lorries and all sorts of equipment. We had only about 10 men in the Canteen all evening".

Soon after that, the Canteen was closed.

4. ITALIAN PRISONERS-OF-WAR

After the Canadians left the camp, it was prepared to receive Italian prisoners-of-war.   A large number of Italian soldiers had been captured in North Africa and shipped to Britain and other countries.   In January 1941 some 130,000 were brought to Britain; and more continued to arrive in 1942 and into 1943.   The Banstead Wood Camp was used to house some 150 of these from 1944 onwards.

The camp area was surrounded by a wire fence and a sentry box was installed at the entrance from Holly Lane.   The old house was taken over for use by the British Sergeant or Sergeant-Major who would be in charge of the camp with his small staff.   The camp was to be one of a number of camps in Surrey and Middlesex under the command of a military headquarters unit set up at a large house called "Westonacres" at Woodmansterne.   The unit was called No. 239 Italian Labour battalion (or 239 ILB).

Italian POWs in Britain, especially after the official surrender by the Italian government in July 1943, were not regarded as prisoners to be rigorously confined, but more as a much-needed source of agricultural labour.   Some 7,000 were billeted on farms, where they both lived and worked.   Others, like those in the Banstead Wood Camp, were accommodated in camps from which they were taken out daily in small parties to work on farms or at other jobs.

Although they were officially restricted in their movements out of the camp apart from these working expeditions, the restrictions were never very severe.   People remember them wandering freely in the areas around the camp, and on warm days sitting on Park Downs, in the woods, and in the fields of Perrotts Farm.

13.

Their stay in the camp temporarily lowered the population of a type of snail to be found in the area of the camp. These edible snails, appropriately known as "Roman snails", were collected by the Italian POWs. to supplement their camp rations.

Stella had an embarrassing experience when walking her little Corgi dog on Park Downs at this time. It happened that the dog's name was Carlo; and when she called out to him, she recalls, a number of Italians with the same name "hove up"!

The outstanding impression left in people's memories of the Italian POWs seems to be of two things - their affection for children, to whom they loved to talk; and the fact that they were always singing. They sang on trucks which took them to and from the workplace, and they sang in the camp itself. Most accounts describe them as singing operatic arias - though probably they were singing Italian popular songs as well.

The question of release and repatriation of prisoners-of-war in Britain was the subject of debate from the end of the war in Europe, both for humanitarian reasons and because of the sheer number of prisoners involved. In June 1945, a month after the ending of hostilities in Europe, there were 118,000 Italian POWs in this country, and 207,000 Germans.

The other side of the coin was that from 1941 onwards the Italians had provided much-needed labour, particularly in agriculture and forestry, and from the autumn of 1944 many of the Germans also had been so employed.

A programme of repatriation of Italian POWs began in the autumn of 1945. POW labour was still valuable for agriculture and for reconstruction work in 1946 - on housing sites, repairing war-damaged houses, roadmaking, sewer and reservoir construction and so on. But with the gradual return of men from the British Armed Forces, the need was progressively lessening. On the other hand, the total number of POWs in Britain threatened actually to increase as POWs were brought back from U.S.A. and Canada, where they had originally been sent. The repatriation of Italians therefore became more urgent; and in May 1946 all the Italians in Banstead Wood camp were taken off to a repatriation camp at Kew Gardens en route for home.

5. THE GERMAN PRISONERS-OF-WAR

The camp at Banstead was at once re-occupied as a "working camp" or "hostel" for about 150 German POWs, and the unit became No. 239 German Working Camp (239 GWC). We have detailed information about this phase of the camp's life both from outside and inside the perimeter. Inside the camp was Mr. Emil Hergesell, a soldier in the German Army who was a prisoner in the camp from May 1946 until he was repatriated in December 1947.

Mr. John Havers, then a Sergeant in the British Army, was posted to the headquarters unit at Woodmansterne just in time to take part in the evacuation of the Italians from the camp and the reception there of the Germans; and Mr. Norman Scott lived in one of the cottages in Holly Lane adjoining the camp from January 1947 onwards until well after the camp was finally closed. The German Camp Doctor's hut was very near the end of his garden, and he often talked with the Doctor, who spoke good English.

German POW's in the Camp.

PoW - Working Camp
239 G - Banstead/ Surrey
ENGLAND 1946
links:- rechts: Ganssen W, Gross W, Hermann L, Grosche H, Hartung K
Gutenberger W, Grosse H, Hergesell Gruner Hf
Grumbach W, Hartmann W, Haag H, Hendrich O,
Hinkel Werner, Hartung Toni, Haeffner Joch,

Oktober 46 - B 10/ D776604

Mr. Hergesell's experiences as a prisoner-of-war were typical of many of his comrades in the camp. Wounded and taken prisoner in Southern France in 1944, he was shipped off to Naples on a hospital ship, and then to the United States, where he was in several camps in different parts of the country. Generally the POWs were kept under strict guard in these camps, but they were well housed and very well fed. Shipped to England in May 1946, they arrived at the Banstead Wood camp after a short transitional stay at a camp in Sheffield.

They were far from happy at the state in which they found the huts and barns which were to form their living and eating quarters in the camp. So they set to work with a will to make them as clean and as comfortable as they could.

They found that, whilst the accommodation and food was much inferior to that in the U.S.A., the camp regime was more easy-going. The fence was no real obstacle; and in place of the guards with sub-machine guns in the American camps, the armed guard at the Banstead camp consisted of one elderly soldier with an old Lee Enfield rifle.

As in the time of the Italian POWs, the old house was occupied by the small British staff - normally a sergeant and a couple of other men. There were a number of living huts and storage huts, including several Nissen huts of what was then a familiar type. Some of the huts were between Holly Lane and the old house, and more behind the old house up to and beyond the line of the Long Barn. Others lay between the Long Barn and the two cottages in Holly Lane, which were outside the camp.

Part of the Long Barn was used as the camp kitchen, whilst the remainder was used as the dining hall. At the end of the Barn was a building which the Germans adapted for use as a camp theatre. The field between the Long Barn and the woods was the Parade Ground, where regular camp parades were held.

There was a German Camp Leader (or Lagerfuhrer), a Sergeant-Major, who was in effect in charge of day-to-day administration and discipline of the POWs in the camp. Besides their own doctor, they had their own camp police, cooks, a shoemaker, medical orderly and so on.

The German cooks did not always know how to make the most of the ingredients available. Sugar and sweeteners were in very short supply. On the other hand, in the canteen syrup of figs was on sale - something which they knew nothing about. One cook had the idea of using the syrup for the puddings which he was making for the POWs. This had the effect of putting the camp latrines under heavy pressure for the next 24 hours!

The British Sergeant for the most part left the POWs to run the camp in their own fashion. The prisoners were in the early days disgruntled, because they had been led to believe before they left the U.S.A. that they were on their way home; but strict German discipline ensured that in general there was little trouble with them, inside the camp or elsewhere.

At first, the POWs were not allowed to leave the camp except when taken out on working parties, and these for the first three months were accompanied by an armed guard. After that, the working parties were taken out and brought back by civilian drivers, and there was no military supervision at the worksites. Occasionally the POWs were allowed out for walks in the woods and fields near the camp, accompanied by one soldier with a rifle.

The working parties were employed on a number of different jobs and at various places within the area allotted to the Woodmansterne H.Q. Unlike the Italians, the Germans at the Banstead Wood Camp were not mainly employed on farm work, though some did work on the North Looe smallholdings near the Drift Bridge.

Their work on preparation of building sites, construction of roads and sewers, repair of war-damaged houses and so on took them as far as Twickenham, Teddington and New Addington. They also worked in Richmond Park, where they cut down old trees and planted new ones. (It was a point of principle between those who went to the Park in winter months that each would bring back to the Camp a couple of logs from the felled trees, to feed the stoves in the huts). Eventually they went even further afield. Mr. Hergesell spent one day in Hyde Park, where he had little to do except a little tidying up.

In the Banstead area, two of the jobs which they did were the preparation of a site in Fir Tree Road for "prefab" houses, and the extension of Shrubland Road (up till then a dead end, about half its present length) to join with Lyme Regis Road and on to Pound Road.

By the end of 1946 there seems to have been little left of the hostile feelings which had been displayed towards German POWs in this country during the critical years of the war. There was still officially a ban on "fraternisation" with POWs; but it is quite clear from the recollections of residents of Banstead that this was being largely ignored in practice.

Now that the war had been over for some time, the POWs in this country were regarded by most people with a good deal of sympathy because they were still in peacetime "fed up and far from home". POWs out on working parties met with friendly acts, and those on farms often became almost part of the farming household.

A campaign was being waged in Parliament by Richard Stokes, M.P., to speed up repatriation of POWs. Some 650 German POWs had in fact by February 1946 been sent back to Germany to help in reconstruction work there; and in September 1946 the Government agreed that the repatriation of all POWs should be carried out "as soon as reasonably practicable". This was bound to be a slow process. Very large numbers of men were involved, and there were great shortages of housing, food and jobs in Germany, which would be aggravated by an extra large influx. The plan was for 15,000 POWs to be sent home each month.

For the POWs in the Banstead Wood Camp awaiting their turn for repatriation, Christmas 1946 seems to have marked the beginning of much greater freedom, officially as well as in practice. At Christmas restrictions were lifted to enable POWs to visit families in the district and to spend some of Christmas with them. They also received visitors in the camp.

The Salvation Army band went to the camp to play for them; and a Roman Catholic priest from St. Aidan's Church in Coulsdon visited the camp, taking with him his young cousin (a girl 11 years old) and one of her friends. That cousin (now Mrs. Atkins) recalls that the camp building into which they went seemed warm and pleasant, and that there were cooking smells - she thinks they were cooking a goose - and a fine Christmas tree. The Germans were extremely friendly, and gave the children sweets.

"Non-fraternisation" was by now virtually a dead letter, and it was soon officially abandoned. The POWs were also given freedom of movement in their spare time within five miles of the camp, on condition that they returned before 8 o'clock in the evening. So men in the Banstead camp could go to Sutton or Croydon on the bus, but they were not allowed to go to London.

They would be recognised outside the camp by the coloured disc - yellow or red or green - sewn on their dark uniforms. On occasion this could give rise to misunderstanding. When POWs from the camp were clearing snow from the High Street, one lady complained to the local policeman about "convicts" being employed in the village, and he had to explain to her that they were "not that sort of prisoner". This was in January 1947, when there were very heavy falls of snow. Besides clearing snow from their camp area, some of the POWs had been sent up to the High Street, where, under strict commands of their Sergeant-Major, they cleared away the snow with a speed and efficiency which a bystander says he never saw before or since!

One effect of the increased freedom of movement was to make it possible for POWs to visit and get to know people in the district. The Society of Friends at Sutton appointed one of their members, who had worked in Germany and spoke fluent German, as a regular Camp visitor. He was usually driven down from Banstead to the camp by Mr. Ken Bulleid, also a member of the Society, who at the time lived in Sandersfield Road. The Society arranged home visits by the prisoners; and sometimes they lent them bicycles, so that they could travel round within the permitted distance. The prisoners were provided with a note stating the name and address of the owner of the cycle, and confirming that permission had been given to use the cycle, in case they were stopped by the police.

Following the heavy falls of snow in January 1947, the POWs mingled with the public in tobogganing down Park Downs opposite the camp. The Germans made their own toboggans from some old Army beds which they found in one of the storehouses.

Mr. Bulleid and his wife offered hospitality to two German POWs at Christmas 1946, and during 1947 they continued to receive them and a number of other POWs at their home. One of these was Henri Heide, whose home was in Mainz. He was not in the Banstead camp but was working as a cook at the Woodmansterne H.Q. For more than 40 years after he had returned to Mainz, a friendship continued between the Bulleids and Henri Heide and his wife; and the Bulleids visited them in Germany, where they also met several others who had been prisoners in the Banstead Wood Camp.

This was by no means an isolated instance of continuing friendship. Mr. Havers kept in touch for many years with one of the German POWs who had worked at the Woodmansterne H.Q. - a capable artist who had painted for him a watercolour picture of "Westonacres" which he still has.

Another POW who was an accomplished artist was Bernhard Piper, one of those befriended by Mr. and Mrs. Bulleid. He was very anxious to visit the National Gallery in London. This was against the rules; but the Bulleids decided to take him there one Sunday in their car. To cover up his POW uniform, they borrowed a long overcoat for him - and the visit was safely accomplished, much to his pleasure.

A lot of the POWs made use of their liberty of movement to do odd jobs for people in their spare time. In the camp they were paid the equivalent of a shilling (5p) a day in "lager gelt" (camp money) - tickets which could be used to buy in the camp canteen what little was available there - a few cigarettes, the inevitable yellow NAAFI cake, and so on. Now they could earn English money to buy things for themselves or to take home with them when they were repatriated. There were plenty of offers of jobs to be done, and these might fetch them five or ten shillings. For instance some worked in the evenings at Park Farm in High Road, Chipstead, and others at the laundry in Chipstead Road, Banstead.

One job taken on by Mr. Hergesell and another POW was to clear an orchard for a lady at Carshalton and prune her apple trees. She told them to take as many apples as they liked, and gave them a bag to take them back to camp.

As they worked, a small boy poked his head through the fence and said, "Hello Germans". They talked to him and gave him some of the apples, and he called his sister to come out and chat with them. Although she had no knowledge of German, and their English was limited to what they had picked up whilst in America, the "conversation" flourished. So did the friendship between her and Emil Hergesell. He visited the house and got to know her family, and by the time in December 1947 when he was released and returned to Germany, the two of them decided that he would come back and they would be married. Indeed, through the efforts of the future Mrs. Hergesell, permission for his return was obtained from the Home Office; and the wedding took place. Some years later Mr. Hergesell became manager of Preedys shop in Banstead High Street, a position he held for 19 years.

The Hergesells' romance was only one of the many between German POWs and English girls at this time. Until July 1947, a ban on marriages between POWs and English girls was in force; but after it was lifted, nearly 800 such marriages took place. More than 16,000 German POWs also obtained permission to take up residence in this country. Meanwhile the programme of repatriation continued, though it was not until July 1948 that the Secretary of State for War was able to announce that it had practically been completed.

The Germans in Banstead Wood Camp left in groups to return to Germany in the later months of 1947. The camp was then left empty for some time, during which the children in the cottages had the run of the camp, and even put on their own shows in the camp theatre.

6. CONCLUSION

The Banstead Woods were officially reopened to the public on the 5th of April 1947 by the Rt. Hon. J. Chuter Ede, M.P., a Government minister with strong Epsom connections.   The mansion in the woods was eventually embodied in a Children's Hospital, as planned before the War.   The official opening took place on the 28th of June 1948.   (It is now the Queen Elizabeth Hospital).

As for Park Farm and the rest of the campsite, after some delay the Banstead Urban District Council bought the property.   They granted a lease of the Long Barn extension and the field at the back to the Boy Scouts Association.   The remainder of the site was converted for use as a Council depot.   The old house near Holly Lane and nearly all the wartime huts were demolished.   Later some more cottages were built adjoining Holly Lane on the northern side of the entrance road.

Very little trace of the camp is now left.   There is a short flight of steps to the right of the Long Barn, which used to lead to the Nissen huts; and the two sheds in front of the Long Barn extension are on the sites of wartime huts, and may well be altered versions of those huts.   It is difficult now to imagine what the area looked like during the years of its occupation for military purposes, or to think of the Woods as anything other than a place for peaceful relaxation and pleasure.

SOURCES

Taped interviews with Mr. Havers, Mr. Scott and Mr. Hergesell.

Note of interview with Miss Edna Touzel and talk with Mrs. Elsie Dansey.

Information from Mr. Bulleid, Mrs. Stella Hayward and others.

BOOKS ON POWs IN ENGLAND

Miriam Kochan:	Prisoners of England	(Macmillan 1980).
Reid & Michael:	Prisoner of War	(Hamlyn 1984).
Richard Garrett:	P.O.W.	(David & Charles 1981).